Hearts Find Rest

The Explanation of the

Remembrance for Anxiety and Sadness

Shaykh Abdur Razzaaq al Badr

Table of Contents

Introduction

This book is derived from two lectures of the Shaykh (May Allah protect him) and describes in detail the benefits of remembrance of Allah and also explains the Authentic Hadeeth of the Prophet (peace and blessings of Allah be upon him):

"There is no-one who is afflicted by distress and grief, and says:

'Allahumma inni 'abduka ibn 'abdika ibn amatika naasyati bi yadika, maada fiyya hukmuka, 'adlun fiyya qadaa'uka. As'aluka bi kulli ismin huwa laka sammayta bihi nafsaka aw anzaltahu fi kitaabika aw 'allamtahu ahadan min khalqika aw ista'tharta bihi fi 'ilm il-ghayb 'indaka an taj'al al-Qur'aana rabee' qalbi wa noor sadri wa jalaa' huzni wa dhihaab hamm'

but Allah will take away his distress and grief, and replace it with joy."

The Lecture

All praise is due to Allaah, Lord of everything that exists.

I testify that none has the right to be worshipped except Allaah alone without any partners (associates).

And I testify that Muhammad (peace and blessings of Allah be upon him) is His slave and messenger.

May Allaah send His Peace and Blessings upon him, his family and all of his companions (Sahaabah).

O Allaah, we don't have any knowledge except what You have taught us.

O Allaah, teach us that which will benefit us and increase us in our knowledge.

And rectify for us all our affairs, and do not leave us to our own even for a blink of an eye.

O Allaah, make us from those people who remember You, those who are grateful (*shukr*) towards You, repentant to You, humble and obedient towards You.

O Allaah, accept our repentance (*tawbah*), wash our sins, make our evidence firm, guide our hearts, make our tongues upright and remove the resentment from our hearts.

O Allaah, we ask from you a sound heart and a truthful tongue.

And we ask that you make us of those who are grateful for Your bounties and to worship You in the best manner.

And we ask you to grant us success in what You love and are pleased with, from upright statements and righteous deeds, and to not leave us to ourselves for even a blink of an eye.

You know our weaknesses and shortcomings and there is no movement nor power for us except through You.

O Allaah, in You (alone) we put our trust, and to You (alone) we turn in repentance, and to You is the final return.

The topic of this gathering is concerning the remembrance of Allaah.

Verily, in the remembrance of Allaah do hearts find rest. (Surah al-Ra'd:28)

And the gatherings of the remembrance of Allaah are the best and the purest of gatherings.

It is stated in Saheeh Muslim, from our Prophet (peace and blessings of Allah be upon him) who said:

No group of people gather in one of the Houses of Allaah to recite the Book of Allaah, studying it together, except that tranquility will descend upon them, mercy will engulf them, angels will surround them, and Allaah will make mention of them to those in His presence.

And it is stated in Saheeh Muslim, from the Hadeeth of Mu'awiyah (Allah be pleased with him), who said: The Messenger of Allaah came out to us while we were gathering in the Masjid remembering Allaah.

So he (peace and blessings of Allah be upon him) said: What has made you gather?

They said: We gathered to remember Allaah and what Allaah has favored us with.

He said: By Allaah, nothing has made you gather except this?

They said: By Allaah, nothing has made us gather except this,

He said: By Allaah, verily I didn't ask you to swear as an accusation.

However, Jibreel just came to me and informed me that Allaah is boasting about you to His angels.

Therefore, it is stated in an authentic Hadith from our Prophet, who said that Allaah said: I am with My slave when he remembers Me and his lips move making mention of Me.

And in the Qur'an, Allaah said: Therefore remember Me. I will remember you... (Surah al-Baqarah:152)

And in the Hadeeth al-Qudsi, Allaah said: Whoever remembers Me, I will remember him. Whoever remembers Me in a gathering, I will remember him in a gathering that is better than it.

I say all this to remind myself and my brothers of the blessings of Allaah upon us, that He has facilitated for us this gathering.

And He alone is the Bestower of this bounty without any partners.

So we ask Him Who has favored us with this gathering to make it a gathering that is sincerely seeking His Face, as a benefit for us, that He accepts it from us and that He makes it on our scales of righteous deeds.

And to make what we say and hear in it a proof for us and not against us, to aid us all upon remembering Him, in being grateful towards Him and to worship Him in the best manner.

Allaah says in Surah al-Ra'd:

Verily, in the remembrance of Allaah do hearts find rest. (Surah al-Ra'd:28)

This tremendous verse contains a virtue of the remembrance of Allaah, its tremendous affair, its noble rank and its elevated status.

This means that this verse imparts peace and tranquility.

When we reflect on this merciful verse and the reality of the hearts of people in this worldly life, their hearts are truly complicated and filled with desires, attraction by lust, suspicion, and temptation; leaving no place to rest in the heart except a sense of loss, displeasure, and irritation; in short, restlessness.

That is, this heart feels restless, irritated, and lost where one suffers from suspicion and doubt.

All these are diseases of the heart.

No heart is at peace except with the remembrance of Allah.

If the heart is far from the remembrance of Allah, then it will be susceptible to these diseases.

Verily it is from the tremendous effects of remembrance of Allah, its noble fruits and blessed benefits of the remembrance of Allaah is that it is tranquility for the hearts, rest for the souls and the removal of its worries, unrest and irritation.

So the hearts will not be at rest, nor will it attain comfort and tranquility similar to the remembrance of Allaah.

So the remembrance of Allaah is relief after hardship and ease after difficulty and comfort after sorrow, grief and worry.

And it is the joy of the people of Iman, the comfort of their souls and the tranquility of their hearts.

It is their refuge from every distress and hardship and from every sorrow and concern.

If the heart of the believer is afflicted with a type of distress, worry or sadness, he resorts to the remembrance of Allaah.

So the worries of his heart will be lifted. And the clouds of sorrow, pain and grief will disperse.

And Allaah will replace it with happiness, relief, comfort and tranquility. Remembering Allah has countless benefits and great influence.

By remembering him, the heart and soul are calmed.

Dhikr (remembrance of Allah) brings blessings and prevents evil.

It makes the servant happy and successful in this world and the Hereafter.

The more a servant commits to dhikr, the more his happiness will be integrated.

ٱلَّذِينَ ءَامَنُوا۟ وَتَطْمَئِنُّ قُلُوبُهُم بِذِكْرِ ٱللَّهِ أَلَا بِذِكْرِ ٱللَّهِ تَطْمَئِنُّ ٱلْقُلُوبُ ﴿٢٨﴾

"Those who have believed and whose hearts are assured by the remembrance of Allah. Unquestionably, by the remembrance of Allah hearts are assured."
(13:28)

Thus, tranquility is being happy and at peace, free from worries and distractions; this can be achieved by remembering Allah.
Without remembering Allah, the heart will die.
Abu Musa Al-Ash'ri narrated that the Prophet

(peace and blessings of Allah be upon him) said:
"The example of the one who remembers his Lord and the one who does not remember Him is like a living person and a dead person."
The Prophet (may Allah's peace and blessings be upon him) compared the one who remembers Allah to a living person and the one who does not remember Allah to a dead person.

In a narration in Saheeh Muslim, the Prophet (may Allah's peace and blessings be upon him) said: "The house in which Allah is remembered and the house in which Allah is not remembered are like the living and the dead respectively."

So, the Prophet (peace and blessings of Allah beupon him) gave an example of a house that remembers Allah with the house of a living, and a house that does not remember Allah with the house of a dead (i.e., graves).

When we combine the words of the two hadeeths, we find that there is an analogy between those who remember Allah (remembrance) and fill their houses with the remembrance of Allah (remembrance) and the houses of the living, i.e. houses full of life, and those who do not remember Allah and do not fill their houses with the remembrance of Allah with the houses of the dead, as if their chests were graves for their hearts, in which there is no real life, but animalistic life.

So, the heart is divided into:

A healthy heart

"Except those who come to Allah with a clean heart (free from shirk, that is polytheism, and nifaq, that is hypocricy)." [Surat Ash-Shu'ara' 26:89].

A healthy heart is the kind of heart that is free from disease and ill will.

It is purified for the sake of Allah, and its deeds are cleansed.

Thus, this heart relies only on Allah, does not depend on other than Him, and performs worship only to Allah.

If it loves, it loves for the sake of Allah, if it hates, it hates for the sake of Allah, if it supports, it supports for the sake of Allah.

This is a clean heart, empty of disease and lust.

It is closer to Allah (the Most High), remembers Him, and worships only Him.

The second type: a dead heart.

This is a heart that turns away from his Lord and Creator and worships another.

A heart that does not carry out His commandments, does not worship, does not remember, does not do good deeds, asks others (other than Allah) in a state of hope, fear, love and hate.

It directs its worship and good deeds to other than Allah. This is a dead heart.

The third type of heart: the heart that has both life and death.

The heart is filled with life when it is honest, sincere, tawheed (worship of Allah alone), and desires to worship Allah, whereas it is lifeless when it is filled with lust and suspicion.

The heart is qualified as dead or alive according to the dominant impulse.

The life of the heart will continue when one keeps close to Allah and remembers Allah with his heart and tongue, whereupon suspicion and lust will disappear.

If one does not remember Allah, then more ugliness and sickness will reside.
"Verily, it is only in the remembrance of Allah that the heart is tranquil."
How can this heart find tranquility? By obeying Allah, relying on Him and asking Allah alone.

Whoever asks Allah alone, hopes in Allah alone, fears Allah alone, relies on Allah alone, depends on Allah alone, relies on Allah alone in everything, then his heart will be at ease with the remembrance of Allah, because he has practiced tawhid and obedience to Allah.

And the heart was only created to remember
Allaah.

So if it becomes heedless of the remembrance
of Allaah, worries will continually come to him.

And it will not be removed from his heart until
he returns his heart to the remembrance of
Allaah.

Therefore, if you were to contemplate upon the
overall supplications for distress that are
narrated from the Prophet, you would find that
all of it returns back to this affair.

Verily the worries will not be lifted from the
heart nor will the grief be removed from it
unless it is occupied with the remembrance of
Allaah

And being heedless from His remembrance is a
tremendous disease, a destruction for the
individual and it is harmful to him.

O brothers and sisters! Pay attention to how
the Messenger of Allah (peace and blessings of

Allah be upon him) healed people who were afflicted with sadness, distress, and anxiety, so that we can appreciate the value of the healing given by the Messenger of Allah with the *dhikr* (remembrance) of Allah.

We all know that a person can be afflicted with sadness, distress, and anxiety.

According to scholars, the heart can be afflicted with these diseases, one of which is related to the past (sadness), another to the present (distress), and a third to the future (anxiety).

Sadness is related to the past; one feels sad when goals are not achieved. For example, one wants to make a deal, but fails, which causes the heart to develop greater feelings of sadness.

Distress occurs when a person feels dissatisfied with his or her current situation.

If a person is worried about his future, he may be anxious.

These ailments cannot be cured except by remembering Allah, and the heart cannot find peace without Allah's help.

Unfortunately, O my brother, when many people are afflicted with grief, distress, and anxiety, they try to cure them without relying on Allah and not remembering Him.

However, some people do things that cause distress and sadness, thinking that it will comfort the heart and relieve sorrow. The heart cannot find peace with bad deeds; only to Allah is the proper place for its return.

How can distress, sadness, and anxiety be cured?

Consider the Prophet's words about the cure of these diseases.

The Prophet (peace and blessings of Allah be upon him) said:

اللَّهُمَّ إِنِّي عَبْدُكَ ابْنُ عَبْدِكَ ابْنُ أَمَتِكَ نَاصِيَتِي بِيَدِكَ ، مَاضٍ فِيَّ حُكْمُكَ ، عَدْلٌ فِيَّ قَضَاؤُكَ أَسْأَلُكَ بِكُلِّ اسْمٍ هُوَ لَكَ سَمَّيْتَ بِهِ نَفْسَكَ أَوْ أَنْزَلْتَهُ فِي كِتَابِكَ ، أَوْ عَلَّمْتَهُ أَحَدًا مِنْ خَلْقِكَ أَوِ اسْتَأْثَرْتَ بِهِ فِي عِلْمِ الْغَيْبِ عِنْدَكَ

أَنْ تَجْعَلَ الْقُرْآنَ رَبِيعَ قَلْبِي ،
وَنُورَ صَدْرِي ، وَجَلاءَ حُزْنِي ،
وَذَهَابَ هَمِّي

"If a Muslim is afflicted with a calamity and he recites this supplication, it will be answered:

O Allah, I am Your servant, the son of Your servant, the son of Your maidservant. My forelock is in Your hand, Your command concerning me is forever executed Your decree over me is just. I ask You with every *Asmaul Husna* (Beautiful Name) that You have described for Yourself, or that You have revealed in Your Book, or that You have taught to one of Your creatures, or that You have chosen to keep in the knowledge of the unseen with You, to make the Qur'an the delight of my heart, the light of my chest, and to relieve my sadness and remove my anxiety."

The Prophet (peace and blessings of Allah be upon him) said: "If he says it, then Allah will take away his sadness and replace it with joy and happiness."

They said, "O Messenger of Allah, should we not learn it?"

The Prophet (peace and blessings of Allah be upon him) said: Yes, whoever hears it should know it."

So, sadness, distress, and anxiety can be replaced with happiness.

But how can this heart be happy?

Saying these prayers (these words of remembrance and supplications) without thinking about their meaning will be meaningless because these *dhikr* and prayers deserve deep thought.

When a person is afflicted with sadness, distress, and anxiety, he should mention it starting with,

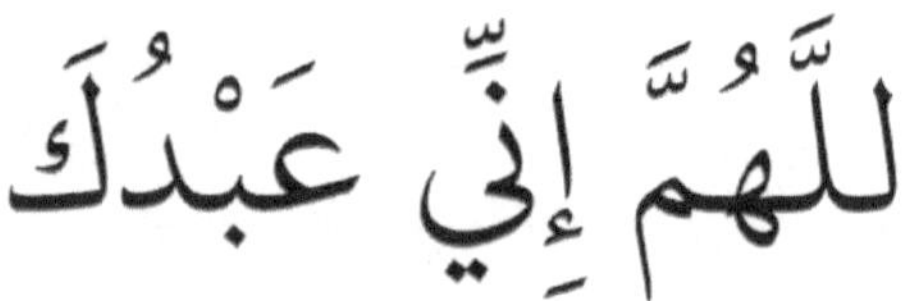

"O Allah! I am Your servant."

This is an acknowledgment that he is a servant of Allah (the Most High), who is His Creator and Sustainer. Servant means a worshipper who obeys Allah's commands.

للَّهُمَّ إِنِّي عَبْدُكَ ابْنُ عَبْدِكَ ابْنُ أَمَتِكَ

"O Allah, I am Your servant, the son of Your servant, the son of Your maidservant."

I am Your servant, and my father's (father, grandfather, and so on) up to Adam (peace be upon him) are Your servants, we are all Your servants and You are our Creator, Lord and Sustainer.

"My forelock is in Your hand,"

forelock is the forehead.

I do not own anything except by Your will and Power.

If You want me to live, I will live.

If You want me to be happy, I will be happy.

If You want me to be healthy, I will be healthy.

If You want me to be rich, I will be rich.

If You want other things like sickness, poverty, I will be sick and poor.

My forelock is in Your hands, and Your Will and Power govern all things.

"Your commandment over me is forever executed."

Your decision will prevail without anyone being able to object because Allah's will is sure. No one can overturn His decision.

What Allah wills will happen and what He does not will, will not happen.

"Your decision for me is just."

O Allah, You are the Just One. He does no injustice, not even the weight of an atom (or a tiny ant), and everything He decides is just.

Then a person invokes Allah with the Asmaul Husna (Beautiful names) and His great attributes.

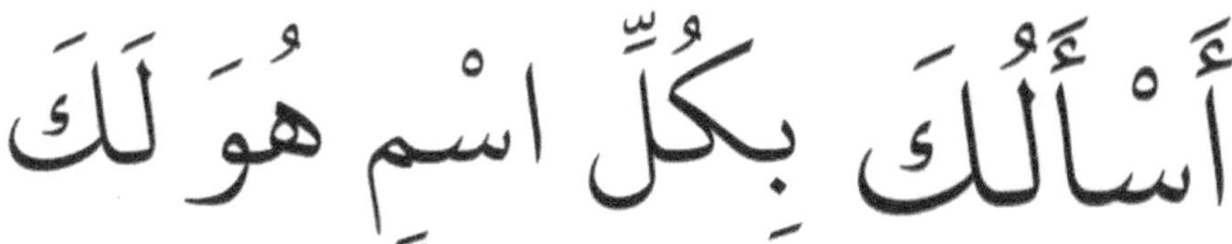

أَسْأَلُكَ بِكُلِّ اسْمٍ هُوَ لَكَ

"I call upon You with every asmaul husna that You have used to describe Yourself."

أَسْأَلُكَ بِكُلِّ اسْمٍ هُوَ لَكَ

It means O Allah, I invoke You with all the asmaul husna.

It is known that the best way to pray to Allah is with His Asmaa' and Attributes. Allah says:

وَلِلَّهِ ٱلْأَسْمَآءُ ٱلْحُسْنَىٰ فَٱدْعُوهُ بِهَا ۖ وَذَرُوا۟ ٱلَّذِينَ يُلْحِدُونَ فِىٓ أَسْمَـٰٓئِهِ ۚ سَيُجْزَوْنَ مَا كَانُوا۟ يَعْمَلُونَ ﴿١٨٠﴾

And to Allah belong the Most Beautiful Names, so invoke Him by them. And leave [the company of] those who practice deviation (or utter impious speech) concerning His names. They will be recompensed for what they have been doing. (Al-A'raf 7:180)

Therefore, the servant calls upon Allah with His Most
Beautiful Names.

أَسْأَلُكَ بِكُلِّ اسْمٍ هُوَ لَكَ

سَمَّيْتَ بِهِ

نَفْسَكَ أَوْ أَنْزَلْتَهُ فِي كِتَابِكَ ، أَوْ

عَلَّمْتَهُ أَحَدًا مِنْ خَلْقِكَ أَوِ

اسْتَأْثَرْتَ بِهِ فِي عِلْمِ الْغَيْبِ عِنْدَكَ

"I ask You with every Asmaul Husna (Beautiful Name) that You have described for Yourself, or that You have revealed in Your Book, or that You have taught to one of Your creatures, or that You have chosen to keep in the knowledge of the unseen with You,"

Then the servant requests:

"To make the Qur'an the delight of my heart."

What is in his heart? In his heart there is sadness and anxiety that makes him sick, so he wants to get rid of it in these ways,

then he asks Allah, "Make the Qur'an the delight of my heart", make me busy with the Qur'an, make my heart full of the Qur'an.

When the heart is occupied with the Qur'an, then there will be no sadness, no distress, no anxiety because there is no place for these diseases.

Sadness, distress, and anxiety cannot find their way into his heart because his heart is filled with the remembrance of Allah.

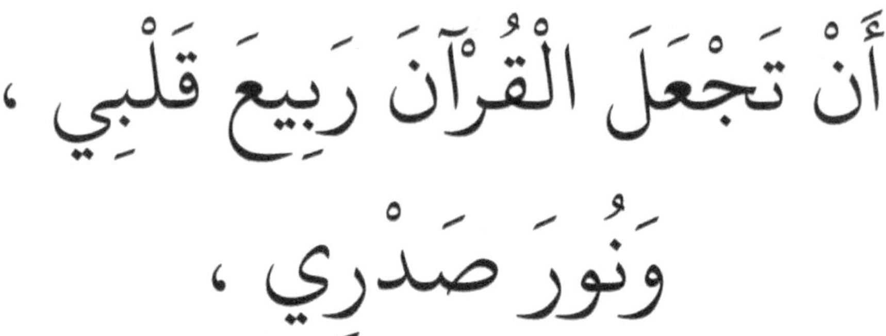

"To make the Qur'an the spring of my heart, the light of my chest."

Note that when the heart is mentioned, he says. "the spring of my heart" and when the chest is mentioned, he says: "the light of my chest."

Thus, he mentions both the spring and the light.

Springs refer to nutrition, plants, life and increase. It is known that the life of the human body and its correct organization arise from the heart.

Likewise, the growth and life of plants and trees comes from its source, so when the heart is improved, the body will also be good.

Thus, the Qur'an is the life of the heart. In this Hadeeth, a person asks Allah to fill his heart with the Qur'ān and the remembrance of Allah so as to remove the diseases in the heart.

"The light of my chest," make a light in my chest by guarding and maintaining the noble Qur'an. This shows that the Qur'an and the remembrance of Allah will make the heart bright.

O brothers and sisters! How can sorrow, distress, and anxiety affect the heart, while the Qur'an is its spring and light? However, weak faith will adversely affect a person so that his heart will be infected with these diseases, which will cause the heart to become restless, suspicious and bored.

أَنْ تَجْعَلَ الْقُرْآنَ رَبِيعَ قَلْبِي ،
وَنُورَ صَدْرِي ، وَجَلَاءَ حُزْنِي ،
وَذَهَابَ هَمِّي

"To make the Qur'an the comfort of my heart, the light of my breast, and take away my sorrow and remove my anxiety."

A person asks Allah to remove sadness from the heart and remove anxiety.

The Prophet (peace and blessings of Allah be upon him) then said:

"Allah will take away his suffering and replace it with joy and happiness."

Shaykh al-Islam Ibn Taymiyyaah, said: Verily, the need of the hearts for the remembrance of Allaah is like the need of a fish for water.

What is the state of a fish if it is separated from water.

You will see in a great state of turmoil.

And this is the state of the hearts. If it is separated from the remembrance of Allaah, it will be in a state of turmoil.

And worries, sorrow and grief will begin to enter into it in accordance to its distance and deviation from the remembrance of Allaah.

Therefore, the remembrance of Allaah is the true life of the hearts. So it doesn't live except by it.

Allaah has said: O you who believe! Answer Allaah and (His) Messenger when he calls you to that which will give you life... (al-Anfal:24)

And He says: Has not the time come for the hearts of those who believe to be affected by Allaah's Reminder, and that which has been revealed of the truth, lest they become as those who received the Scripture before, and the term was prolonged for them and so their hearts were hardened? And many of them were disobedient to Allaah. (al-Hadid:16)

Know that Allaah gives life to the earth after its death! Indeed We have made clear the signs to you, if you but understand. (al-Hadid:17)

Take heed to this example and how excellent it is.

Know that Allaah gives life to the earth after its death... So just as the earth dies, if Allaah sends rain upon it, it is stirred (to life), and it swells and puts forth every lovely kind (of growth).

Likewise is the case for the hearts in its need for the remembrance of Allaah.

And giving concern to the remembrance of Allaah is like the need of the earth and plants for rainfall. If rain is withheld from the earth, it will die.

And likewise, if the remembrance of Allaah, and the greatest of it is the Qur'an, is withheld from the hearts, it will die.

Due to this, Allaah called the revelation in His Book: (*Ruh*).

This is because the true life is only by way of it.

So there is no life for it except by the remembrance of Allaah.

Allaah said: And thus We have sent to you (Ruh) of Our Command.

You knew not what is the Book, nor what is Faith?

But We have made it (this Qur'an) a light wherewith We guide whosoever of Our slaves We will. And verily, you (O Muhammad) are indeed guiding (mankind) to the Straight Path.

The Path of Allaah, to Whom belongs all that is in the heavens and all that is in the earth. Verily, all the matters at the end go to Allaah (for decision). (al- Shurah:52-53)

He said: The Event, ordained by Allaah will come to pass, so seek not to hasten it. Glorified

and Exalted be He above all that they associate
as partners with Him.
He sends down the angels with (Ruh) of His
Command... (al-Nahl:1-2)

And He said: Which the trustworthy (Jibril)
has brought down; (al- Shu'ara:193)

In this verse, Allaah calls Jibril - 'Ruh' because
he descends with the revelation, with it is the
life of the hearts.

So there is no life of the hearts except by the
remembrance of Allaah and the greatest of it is
the Noble Qur'an, the Book of the Lord of all
that exists, which is the life, happiness, success
of the hearts in this life and the next.

And from the affairs of the remembrance of
Allaah regarding the tranquility of the hearts,
is that it expels the Shaytan from the slave.

And the closeness of the Shaytan to the slave
attracts worries, sorrow and fear.

Allaah said: It is only Shaytan that suggests to you the fear of his supporters and friends...
(Ale imran:175)

He said: in order that he may cause grief to the believers.... (al Mujadilah:10)

And he diverts the people from the remembrance of Allaah with his devilish insinuations, whispers and spittle.

Due to this, it is legislated to seek refuge with Allaah from him.

Allaah said:

Say: I seek refuge with the Lord of mankind, the King of mankind, the God of mankind, from the evil of the whisperer who withdraws..
(al-Nas:1-4)

These are two descriptions of the Shaytan: the whisperer, who withdraw...

Indeed, when the individual is heedless of the remembrance of Allaah, he whispers but when the individual remembers Allaah, he withdraws.

So the remembrance of Allaah expels the Shaytan and distances him from the believing slave.

While being heedless from the remembrance of Allaah attracts the Shaytan.

Allaah says: And whosoever turns away from the remembrance of the Most Beneficent, We appoint for him Shaytan to be an intimate companion to him. (al-Zukhruf:36)

When the Shaytan perches over the heart of the slave, he fills it with every trial, and despicable matter, and Allaah's refuge is sought.

And he causes it to fall into severe types of deviation that distances him from the obedience of Allaah.

And much of the sorrow that the hearts are afflicted with are due to the heedlessness of the individual from the remembrance of Allaah. So Shaytan perches over the heart.

So there is no tranquility nor comfort in the heart.

Therefore, from the effects and results of the tranquility which is in the hearts of the people of Iman, by them establishing the remembrance of Allaah, is the repelling of the Shaytan from the heart of the slave.

Shaytan is not able to withstand the remembrance of Allaah.

Haven't you seen what is stated in the Hadith of our Prophet (peace and blessings of Allah be upon him) who said: If the Shaytan hears the Adhan, he flees while passing wind.

Due to the severity of not being able to withstand the remembrance of Allaah.

And the entire Adhan is the remembrance of Allaah

Therefore, the remembrance of Allaah is a fortified fortress for the Muslim which protects him, by the permission of Allaah, from the accursed Shaytan.

It is stated in the Musnad and the Jami' of al-Tirmidhi and other than them from our Prophet (peace and blessings of Allah be upon him) who said:

Yahya ibn Zakariyah (peace be upon him) said to his people: Allaah commanded me with five statements. And He commanded me to command you with them...

So he commanded with Tawhid, the prayer, fasting and giving charity and

then he mentioned the fifth command: And I command you with the remembrance of Allaah. The parable of the one who remembers his Lord is that of a man who sets off while his enemy is pursuing him from behind. So he takes refuge in a fortified fortress and protects himself from him.

So the one who remembers Allaah is like the individual who entered into a fortified fortress protecting him from his enemy.

So the remembrance of Allaah is a fortress for the Muslim.

Due to this, a number of the people of knowledge from the past and present titled their books, regarding the remembrance of Allaah and mentioning the legislated remembrances, with: 'The Fortress'.

This is because in the remembrance of Allaah is a fortress for the Muslim and a protection from the accursed Shaytan, and being safe from his insinuations.

Shaytan's enmity towards the believing slaves of Allaah is continuous. It doesn't stop.

"Then I will come to them from before them and behind them, from their right and from their left, and You will not find most of them as thankful ones (i.e., they will not be dutiful to You)." (al-A'raf:17)

So the Shaytan will come to the slave from every angle.

Imam Ibn al-Qayyim put forth a similitude for the state of the Shaytan with the believing slave regarding him falling into heedlessness and diverting him from the remembrance of Allaah.

The similitude of him is that of a man who has with him a piece of meat and surrounding him is a hungry dog circling him from every angle. Waiting for the slightest moment of heedlessness to snatch his meat.

And this is the state of the Shaytan with the believing slave.

So how dire is the need of the believing slave to continuously be upon the remembrance of Allaah.

When he leaves his house, he remembers Allaah.

بسم الله توكلت على الله

If he says this, it will be said: You been guided, sufficed and protected.

And the Shaytan will tell the other Shaytan: How can you enter upon the slave who has been guided, sufficed and protected?

When he enters the home, he says and mentions the Name of Allaah, then the Shaytan will not be able to enter.

If he enters without mentioning Allaah, Shaytan will say: You have a place to stay. And when you don't mention Allaah before eating, Shaytan will say: You have a place to eat.

And who will accept for himself that Shaytan stays with him in his home and that he sits and eats with him, while he is the most contentious of his enemies and the most severe of his adversaries.

And whoever leaves off mentioning Allaah when he enters the home, then he has given permission to the Shaytan to enter.

And if he leaves off mentioning Allaah before he eats, then he has given permission to the Shaytan to eat with him.

When the Muslim enters into the place where he relieves himself and says:

بسم الله اللهم إني أعوذ بك من الخبث والخبائث

(Search Amazon for "Hisn Al-Muslim" to get the authentic prayer and supplication book) this (the above prayer) is refuge for him from the Shaytan.

As stated in the Hadith: It is the veil of the *Awrah* of the children of Adam from the sight of the Jinn.

So it is a veil for the slave.

If he reads Ayat al-Kursi before he goes to sleep, a protector from Allaah will continue to be with him. And Shaytan will not approach him until the morning.

And the texts regarding this affair are abundant.

Therefore, how dire is the need of the slave to give great concern to the narrated remembrances, regardless if it is from the remembrances that are regularly done at specific times or the unrestricted remembrances.

So he gives concern to the remembrance of Allaah to attain tranquility in his heart, for his soul to be at ease, to be distant from the Shaytan, to establish for himself happiness and peace of mind.

It is stated in the Book of Allaah the command to remember Allaah frequently, due to the dire need of the slave to continually give concern to the remembrance of Allaah.

And from them is the Statement of Allaah:

And the men and the women who remember Allaah much with their hearts and tongues. Allaah has

prepared for them forgiveness and a great reward. (al-Ahzab:35)

Allaah said: O you who believe! Remember Allaah with much remembrance. And glorify His Praises morning and afternoon. He it is Who sends His blessings on you, and His angels too, that He may bring you out from darkness... (al-Ahzab:41-43)

He said: Remember Allaah as you remember your forefathers or with a far more remembrance. (al-Baqarah:200)

And the verses regarding this affair are abundant.

So the slave is in dire need to continuously give concern to the remembrance of Allaah in abundance.

And the virtue of the remembrance of Allaah, its tremendous status, its great rewards and what results in it, from the tremendous good, profound blessings and various benefits, are stated in the Sunnah.

It is stated in the Jami' of al-Tirmidhi from the Hadeeth of Abi Darda who said that the Prophet (peace and blessings of Allah be upon him) said:

Shall I not inform you of what your best and purest actions are before your King, better for you than you meeting your enemy, striking their necks and them striking yours, and better than spending gold and silver?

They said: Of course O Messenger of Allaah!

He said: The remembrance of Allaah.

And it is established in the Saheeh from the Hadith of Abu Hurayrah, who said that our Prophet said: The Mufardun have taken the lead.

They said: And who are the Mufardun O Messenger of Allaah?

He said: The men and the women who remember Allaah much with their hearts and tongues.

In this Hadeeth, it is as if can conceptualize the state of the people of Iman as if they are on a racecourse.

The men and the women who remember Allaah much with their hearts and tongues are the ones taking the lead in this racecourse. There is nobody surpassing them except the one that performs their actions and more.

So the people of the remembrance of Allaah are the people who have taken the lead. As our Prophet said: The Mufardun have taken the lead.

The remembrance of Allaah is the objective of every act of worship.

The prayer, fasting, Hajj and other than them from the acts of obedience, were only legislated to establish the remembrance of Allaah.

And establish the prayer for My remembrance. (TaHa:14)

He said: The Tawaf around the House, the Sa'i between Safa and Marwa and the stoning of the Jamarat were only to establish the remembrance of Allaah.

Due to this, the people of worship, from prayer, fasting, Hajj and other than that, their rewards vary depending on their portion of how much they remember Allaah.

It has been stated in a Hasan Hadith (due to other proofs that strengthen it) that our noble Prophet was asked: Which of those that pray is greatest in reward?

He said: The ones who remember Allaah most while praying.

He was asked: Which of the pilgrims are greatest in reward?

He said: The ones who remember Allaah most while performing Hajj.

He was asked: Which of those who fast are greatest in reward?

He said: The ones who remember Allaah most while fasting.

From this Hadith and other than it, the people of knowledge and from them is Ibn al-Qayyim, in his book a tremendous principle regarding the affair of the differentiation of reward in worship.

Verily, the people with the greatest reward in every act of worship are those that remember Allaah the most while performing them.

The people with the greatest reward in every act of worship are those that remember Allaah the most while performing them.

If there are two individuals who fast, one of them busies his day of fasting with the remembrance of Allaah, while the other busies his day or a portion of his day sleeping, is the fasting of the two the same?

Is the prayer of a slave who fills the beginning and the end of his prayer with the remembrance of Allaah, with his heart and tongue, inwardly and outwardly while another individual who stands in his prayer with his body, while his heart is either in its own galaxy, or thinking about his work or other than that from his affairs.

Are their prayers the same?

The appearance of their actions are the same. However, the difference between the two actions regarding reward, is like the difference between the heavens and the earth.

So the people with the greatest reward in every act of obedience are those that remember Allaah the most while performing them.

The remembrance of Allaah is done with the heart and the tongue.

And this is the highest and loftiest level of the remembrance of Allaah.

The scholars have mentioned that the remembrance of Allaah has three levels.

The first is the remembrance of Allaah with the heart and the tongue, which is the highest level.

After is the remembrance of Allaah with just the heart and then its the remembrance of Allaah with just the tongue.

And the highest level of the remembrance of Allaah is when the heart and tongue of the person is involved in the remembrance of Allaah.

And from the greatest means that will assist one in this is contemplating upon and understanding the meanings of the legislated remembrances.

And this is an affair that many people are heedless of.

And the Salaf have mentioned the importance of giving concern to the meanings of the remembrances and what they guide to.

Many of the people utter the words of the remembrance of Allaah or the legislated supplications without understanding what they mean.

And the benefit for the slave is only established completely when he gives concern to understanding the meanings of the remembrances and what they guide to.

We will contemplate over this beneficial story, which is the story of Fudhay ibn Iyadh which is narrated by Abu Nu'aym in al-Hilya in the biography of Fudhayl.

Fudhayl saw a man who had some negligence in him.

So he asked him: How old are you?

He responded: I'm sixty years old.

He said: Do you know that you are on a path
and you are about to reach its end?

So the man said:

انا لله و انا اليه راجعون

(Inna Lillaahi wa inna ilayhi raajioon)

So he responded to him: Do you know the
explanation of this statement?

And this is the point of reference.

Do you know the explanation of this
statement?

Meaning, do you know the meaning of your
statement:

انا لله و انا اليه راجعون

Look at the statement being said during the
time of the Tabi'in.

Do you know the explanation of this statement?

So he said: And what is the explanation of this statement?

Many people say the words. They say:

لا حول و لا قوة الا بالله

(Laa Hawla wa-laa quwata illaa billaah.) However, if you asked what does it mean, they will say: I don't know.

So one says:

انا لله و انا اليه راجعون

(Inna Lillaahi wa inna ilayhi raajioon) If it was said to him: What is its meaning? He would say: I don't know.

Likewise is the case with many of the remembrances and the legislated supplications.

So he responded to him: Do you know the explanation of this statement? He

said: What is its explanation?

He said:

انـا لله

(Inna lillaah)Meaning, I am a slave to Allaah.

و انا اليه راجعون

(wa inna ilayhi raajioon)
Meaning, and to Him I will return.

So if you know that you are a slave to Allaah and that you will return to Him, then know that He will question you.

And if you know that He will question you, then prepare the answers for the questions.

So he said: So what is the solution?

Fudhayl said: It is easy.

"Do good from what is left in your life, and what has preceded will be forgiven. Indeed, if you were to do evil from what is left in your life, you will be punished for what has preceded and for what is left in your life."

We derive an extremely lofty piece of benefit from this tremendous story in regards to giving concern to the meanings of the remembrances and what they guide to.

Therefore, actualizing their meanings, from sincerity, glorification and exaltation for Allaah the Blessed and Most High, or seeking aid and refuge, and relying upon Him, or other than that from what the legislated remembrances comprises, from the tremendous and blessed meanings.

And the scholars have said: The slave uttering the words of the remembrances without knowing its meanings will have little benefit and little impact if there even is any effect.

And the greatest calamity is when an individual utters the words of the legislated remembrances and nullifies it with his actions.

And this is a tremendous calamity.

To the extent that there are individuals who say:

لا اله الا الله

(Laa Ilaaha Illal-laah)
And then when they raise their hands to supplicate, they say: Help me O so and so!

They then seek refuge in other than Allaah.

So seeking refuge in other than Allaah in his supplication nullifies his statement:

لا اله الا الله

This is because he said it without understanding what it means, from Tawhid and sincerity to Allaah.

Indeed

لا اله الا الله

is the greatest remembrance as our Prophet (peace and blessings of Allah be upon him) said:

The greatest remembrance is

لا اله الا الله

And it is the highest branch of Iman as he said:

Iman has seventy some odd branches. The highest of them is the statement

لا اله الا الله

And it is the most elevated of what Islam is built upon.
So when it is found in the people those that utter these statements of the legislated remembrance without understanding their meanings, you'll find in some of their actions that which nullifies and opposes these statements.

When an individual doesn't know the meanings and what it (the remembrance of Allah and the prayers) guides to, he falls into various mistakes and from them is that he makes some of the remembrance in places that are inappropriate for it.

Returning to what we began with, and with it we conclude this gathering.

Allaah says: Verily, in the remembrance of Allaah do hearts find rest.
(al-Ra'd:28)

And this tranquility that is in the hearts due to the remembrance of Allaah s is not by merely saying them with just the tongue.

Rather tremendous concern must be given to understanding the meaning of the remembrances and understanding what they guide to and striving against the soul in establishing what they guide to, from Tawhid, magnification, glorifying, sanctifying Allaah, the Blessed and Most High, or seeking aid, relying upon Him, or other than that from the tremendous meanings and lofty objectives that the remembrances comprise

And we ask Allaah by His beautiful Names and lofty Attributes to benefit us in what He has taught us, to increase us in knowledge, to rectify all our affairs and to not leave us to our own for a blink of an eye.

O Allaah, rectify our religion of which our affairs are protected, rectify for us our worldly life where our life exists, rectify for us our Hereafter which is our resort to which we have to return.

And make our lives an increase to perform all types of good, and make death a comfort for us from every evil.

O Allaah, forgive us all our sins, great and small, the first and the last, those that are apparent and those that are hidden.

O Allaah, forgive us and our parents, the male and female Muslims, the male and female believers, those that are alive and those that are deceased.

O Allaah, give our soul its Taqwa, purify it, You are the best of those that purify. You are its Ally and its Master.

O Allaah, we ask You for guidance, Taqwa, chastity and contentment.

O Allaah, we ask you for steadfastness in all our affairs and determination in following the right path. We ask You for what will obligate Your Mercy and Forgiveness.

We ask you to make us thankful for Your blessings and to make us worship You properly. We ask you for a sound heart and a truthful tongue.

We ask you for the best of what You know and we seek refuge in You from the worst of what you know and We seek Your forgiveness for what You know. Indeed You are the All-Knower of the unseen.

O Allaah help us and do not give help against us. Grant us victory and do not grant victory over us. Plot for us and do not plot against us. Guide us and make right guidance easy for us.

Grant us victory over those who act wrongfully towards us.

O Allaah, make us from those who remember You, those who are grateful towards You, repentant to You, humble and obedient towards you.

O Allaah, accept our repentance, wash our sins, establish our evidence, guide our hearts, make our tongues upright and remove the malice from our hearts.

O Allaah, our Lord, distance us and the
Muslims from the trials and tribulations that
which is apparent and that which is hidden.

O Allaah, rectify what is between us, unite our
hearts, guide us to the path of peace and take
us from the darkness to the light.

And bless us in our hearing and our sight, our
wives and our children, our wealth and our
time and rectify all of our affairs O Lord of all
that exists.

O Allaah, apportion for us fear which would
serve as a barrier between us and your
disobedience, and obedience which would take
us to Your Paradise; and certainty which would
ease for us the calamities of this world.

O Allaah! let us enjoy our hearing, our sight and our power as long as You keep us alive and make our heirs from our own offspring, and make our revenge restricted to those who oppress us, and support us against those who are hostile to us. Let no calamity afflict our religion. Let not worldly affairs be our main concern, or the limit of our knowledge. Let not those rule over us be those who do not show us mercy.

O Allaah, glory and praise be to You. I testify that none has the right to be worshipped besides You. I seek Your forgiveness and repent to You.

May Allaah send His Peace and blessings upon Your slave and messenger, our Prophet Muhammad, upon his family and his companions.

www.ingramcontent.com/pod-product-compliance
Lightning Source LLC
Chambersburg PA
CBHW061402160726
47995CB00001B/425